Tantrums

PRACTICAL
parenting

 A Pyramid Parenting Paperback

Tantrums

**Understanding and
coping with your
child's emotions**

Eileen Hayes

hamlyn

An Hachette UK Company
www.hachette.co.uk

A Pyramid Paperback

First published in Great Britain in
2003 by
Hamlyn, a division of Octopus
Publishing Group Ltd
2–4 Heron Quays, London E14 4JP
www.octopusbooks.co.uk
www.octopusbooksusa.com

This edition published in 2009

Distributed in the U.S. and Canada
by Octopus Books USA:
c/o Hachette Book Group
237 Park Avenue
New York NY 10017

This material was previously
published as *Tantrums*

ISBN 978-0-600-61967-3

A CIP catalogue record for this
book is available from the British
Library

Printed and bound in China

10 9 8 7 6 5 4 3 2 1

contents

Introduction   6
A whole book on tantrums?   6
My personal experience   8

1 THE FACTS ABOUT TANTRUMS   10
  • What is a tantrum?   12
  • Research into tantrums   16
  • Don't children just grow out of them?   18

2 UNDERSTANDING YOUR TODDLER   20
  • Just normal!   22
  • More difficult children   24
  • Are boys harder to handle?   26
  • Children who don't have tantrums   28

3 WHAT CAUSES TANTRUMS?   30
  • Tantrum triggers   32
  • Identifying flashpoints   36

4 CAN TANTRUMS BE AVOIDED?   44
  • Avoidance tactics   46
  • Heading off tantrums   48
  • Everyday battlegrounds   52

5 DEALING WITH TANTRUMS   56
  • Handling minor tantrums   58
  • Dealing with public tantrums   60
  • Dealing with major tantrums   64

6 THE POSITIVE APPROACH   68

   • Positive parenting   70

   • Positive discipline   74

   • Making humour work for you   78

7 ACTION PLAN   82

   • Helping your child to mature
     beyond tantrums   84

   • Not happy with your response?   86

   • Helping yourself   88

   • Top ten ways to deal with tantrums   90

   INDEX   94

   ACKNOWLEDGEMENTS   96

Introduction

A whole book on tantrums?

When you first pick up this book, you may be thinking to yourself 'How can there be a whole book on tantrums? What is there to say about them beyond the obvious?' I must admit, when I first came to write it I had pretty much the same reaction: what could possibly fill all those chapters on a single subject like tantrums? But then I started speaking to parents – some with children right in the middle of the classic ages for having tantrums, some whose children were older but who still remembered how stressful and distressing tantrums had been for a period of their lives, and even a few with older children who were still having them.

I was also very struck by something else. This was often expressed as a joke. One father of three small children said to me 'You want quotes and cases on tantrums? I can fill your book – and that's only the ones by the wife!' Another parent commented, 'I wish I could say I'm a good example to the kids, but I find myself throwing a tantrum when I get really mad about something'. The reality seems to be that, far from being a phenomenon restricted to toddlers during the so called 'terrible twos', tantrums, 'losing it', screaming and yelling when frustrated, and various other forms of bad behaviour are not that uncommon in lots of older children – and more than just a handful of adults!

Robbie is still likely to have tantrums, even though he's 5. He recently got angry and crawled away and huddled into the corner of the bath. He never wants you to be humorous, and holding him tightly doesn't work. Even ignoring him doesn't really work, though he does get the message. Tantrums can certainly take a different twist at this age. Recently, when he got very angry he said, 'I'm leaving home!' He actually put on his coat, forgetting to put his shoes on, and went out to go down the road. I watched him to see what would happen. He stopped, looking as if he was thinking about it, then came back. He said, 'Right, I've decided to come in, but next time I won't!'

Veronica, mother of Daniel (7), Robbie (5) and Natasha (2)

Below *Teach your child to express himself through words not actions.*

My personal experience

I have four children, ranging in age from 10 years right up into the 20s. I generally have very clear memories of their childhoods and my recollections have not been especially whitewashed over time. I still remember the sleepless nights, colicky episodes and various types of behaviour that seemed undesirable at the time.

Above As your child strives to be more independent, he can become easily frustrated.

I also remember well that it can feel quite hard to leave babyhood behind. That amazing stage when your baby relies on you for everything and you are at the centre of the universe is over all too soon. Many parents feel some sense of loss and regret when their baby becomes a child – and somehow tantrums have a way of impressing on you rather forcibly that the baby days are gone!

Yet I just don't remember tantrums being much of a problem with any of my children. This is not to say that none of them ever had a tantrum, but they were minor stormy episodes that were over very quickly or easily diverted by distraction into something else. I therefore have to confess that I am rather perplexed when I see a child having a major raging tantrum on the floor of the supermarket, or reaching boiling point within minutes of a frustrating event.

So, does this mean that I am doing something secret and marvellous as a 'parenting expert', which has prevented any of my children getting to that point? Or is it just that I have been exceptionally lucky in having children with placid, easily moulded personalities? Well, it's certainly not the latter – my children, just like everybody else's, could sometimes be very challenging indeed. It is also not likely to be the former – just knowing about something and learning the skills to use in a particular situation is only ever part of the picture. In the heat of the moment, when parents are angry, it is only too easy to do things we regret. Instead of putting our knowledge into practice, we revert to the way we have always dealt with a situation, or the way we remember our parents dealing with it. It can be very hard to break out of these familiar patterns.

That is why this book also concentrates on parents. Many say that their children's behaviour is the problem, and that they want to find ways to cut down on their tantrums, but that is only ever part of what needs to change. How you deal with setting limits, controlling your own anger and handling the inevitable stresses of everyday life all have a huge impact on your child's behaviour.

It is important to be realistic and to understand that conflicts and anger are always present in families – or, indeed, whenever one person deals with another. But you can learn how to handle them in a way that will take the power out of tantrums and make your child much less likely to use them.

Both my own experience and everything I have learned about children and parents have convinced me that it is possible to bring up children almost without any bad tantrums at all – but of course it is hard work. Nobody ever said being a parent was easy!

So, if there is anything valuable in the expertise I have gained over many years of reading and learning about being a parent, and in the myriad experiences other parents have shared with me, then I am happy to share it with you in the pages of this book.

Above Think of all the good times you have with your child and remember that tantrums are a normal part of a child's development.

9

the facts about tantrums

1

- What is a tantrum?

- Research into tantrums

- Don't children just grow out of them?

What is a tantrum?

The dictionary definition of a tantrum tells us that it is an 'outburst of bad temper or petulance', and clearly such outbursts can happen at every age. However, when most people talk about tantrums they are thinking about something very specific – the explosive bad temper displayed by young children.

Grace throws herself on the floor and sobs her demands every time I am feeding the baby – it started soon after the baby was born, always when she wants my attention. I feel that she has to learn that you can't have attention immediately. I see tantrums as part of her growing up and becoming a child. Sometimes, though, my resolve weakens – I realize she is upset. I am OK for a few minutes, then I give in, put the baby down, and deal with whatever she wants and comfort her. Then I go back to the baby.

Sarah, mother of Grace (2) and Holly (5 months)

This behaviour is usually worst around 18 months to 3 years of age, still quite common up to 5 or 6, and – or so conventional wisdom goes – not very common and gradually disappearing after that.

Tantrum types

In *Temper Tantrums in Young Children*, psychologist Michael Potegal identified two distinct types of tantrum, each with a different emotional and behavioural basis:
- Anger tantrums are characterized by the child stamping, kicking, hitting and screaming.
- Distress tantrums are characterized by the child crying and sobbing, throwing himself down and running away. Very young children often express sadness or loss as a tantrum.

In their book *Raising Happy Children*, Jan Parker and Jan Stimpson also describe two different tantrum types:
- Tantrums based on frustration and anger.
- Tantrums rooted in confusion and fear.

With Megan, absolutely anything triggers it off, but especially not getting her own way. She stamps her feet and screams hysterically. When we are at home I put her in another room to calm down. She realizes that I am angry and often wants me to come back. She will knock on the door where I am and I ask her if she is ready to calm down.

When we are out it is more difficult to try to reason with her. When she sees something on a shelf and knows she can't have it, it starts her off. One thing that does seem to work is if I tell her that the shop manager is coming – then she will stop! I also hate it if she starts in the car, because I can't really do anything. I often just turn the music up to try and block it out.

Louise, mother of Megan (3)

Left *Tantrums are caused by frustration, anger, confusion and fear.*

Key facts

- Although anger is the emotion that is most obvious to parents, and they often describe episodes as 'temper tantrums', this is almost always combined with another feeling for the child, such as frustration or panic.
- It is a fairly obvious but sometimes forgotten truism that a child doesn't have tantrums when she is on her own. A full-blown tantrum requires an audience. They are almost always conducted in relation to you, the parent, or to someone else with whom the child feels very safe and familiar. It takes two people to create a tantrum, so in that sense they are interactive, not simply reactive.
- The child's temperament does play a part. A more active, strong-willed child may be more likely to have tantrums. Parents usually know from baby days whether they have this type of child. As a baby she may seem to cry and fuss more, or sleep less well than other babies.
- Some estimates say that one in five 2-year-olds have at least two tantrums per day – but remember that this means that four out of five don't.
- Although the phrase 'terrible twos' probably sums up how parents view the strong likelihood of tantrums at that age, and this may be when they are most common, they can start as early as 1 year, and in some cases go on beyond 5 years.
- If handled successfully by parents early on, tantrums are likely to become less common as the child grows older, and the worst is usually over by age 3 or 4 years.
- Tantrums in older children of 4 or 5 are rarely the same impossible-to-control affairs of 2-year-olds. By that age the child is able to talk about her anger and frustration, and work at getting her feelings back under control, so she will not usually have the same need to use tantrums in order to release her emotions.

- Tantrums often happen when a child's feelings are out of control – she may literally 'boil over'. You know that moment when the saucepan of milk starts rising and how even taking it away from the heat won't stop the reaction? That is often how it seems with tantrums.
- An estimated three-quarters of all tantrums happen at home, but the worst tantrums often seem to be saved for public places, ensuring maximum attention for the child and maximum embarrassment for the parent. The classic of the child writhing on the supermarket floor, screaming at the top of her lungs, is a classic simply because it is so universal.
- Behaviours common in tantrums include shouting, screaming, crying, hitting, kicking, stiffening limbs, arching back, dropping on the floor and running away.
- In a really severe tantrum, a child can go blue in the face, be sick, even hold her breath until she is almost unconscious – but natural reflexes will make sure she starts breathing again before coming to any harm.
- Although it may seem to parents that a child is just being difficult deliberately, she will almost never be doing it for that reason. The majority of tantrums are an expression of loss of control though some may involve attempts at manipulation. Tantrums are the child's complicated response to feelings of frustration, helplessness and anger, and happen because of her lack of the skills needed to deal with these feelings.

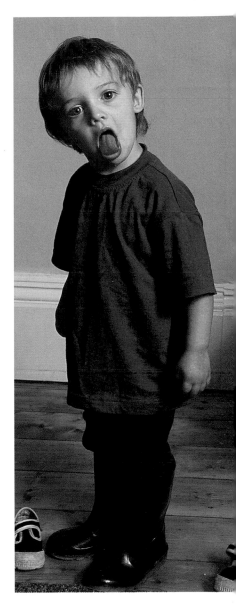

Above By the time a child is 3 or 4 years old, tantrums are far less common.

15

Research into tantrums

Over the years, psychologists and researchers have shown considerable interest in looking at the topic of difficult-to-manage behaviour, including tantrums, in children.

Below *One of the most common causes of tantrums is conflict with parents.*

Questions they have asked include:
- Are tantrums separate from, or part of, generally difficult behaviour?
- What constitutes a severe tantrum?
- Do children just grow out of them?
- How do children and parents act when the tantrum is over?

Key findings
- A number of studies show that tantrums occur at least once a week in 50–80 per cent of pre-school children, suggesting that they are part of normal behaviour.
- Between 5 and 20 per cent of children, depending on the study, have tantrums severe enough to cause concern to parents.
- Studies show that the major cause of toddler tantrums is conflict with parents – most commonly over food and eating (16.7 per cent), closely followed by being put in a pushchair, highchair, car seat and so on (11.6 per cent), then by dressing (10.8 per cent). There are also peaks, with more tantrums occurring in the late morning and early evening, when the child is either hungry or tired.
- Tantrums usually have distinct stages, with warning signs such as demanding attention or 'looking for trouble'. They often end with a sad, sobbing stage and the need for comfort.

- Researchers define severe tantrums as lasting longer than 15 minutes or happening three or more times a day. Using this measure, 6.8 per cent of a sample of 502 children had severe tantrums; just over half of these children with severe tantrums had multiple behavioural problems.
- Some factors that have been linked to increased tantrums are sleep disturbance, speech problems, more illness, maternal stress and depression, and the use of smacking as a method of discipline.
- There may be more tantrums in boys and in relatively deprived homes, but this is not clearly established.
- One survey found that 35 per cent of tantrums ended in a cuddle, and that the child often made the first move to make up with parents.
- Another study noted that self-comforting behaviours such as thumb-sucking or using a soft toy increase after a tantrum.
- In anger tantrums, the behaviours are worse at the start and then tail off. In distress tantrums, they tend to increase over the course of the tantrum.
- Ill-tempered children often become ill-tempered adults, especially in situations involving interpersonal conflicts and requiring negotiations, such as in marriage and parenting.

Below *Children often need a cuddle after an emotional outburst.*

17

Don't children just grow out of them?

Research has also tried to determine whether tantrums have any links to specific adult problem behaviours – for instance, whether there is any association between a particularly hard-to-manage child who has a lot of tantrums at 3 years old, and the subsequent likelihood of episodes of delinquency or violent crime as an adult.

Above Temperament can play a large part in whether or not your child has severe emotional outbursts.

It has already been well established that links exist in this way from middle childhood, for example:
- Surveys have shown that antisocial behaviour from 5 years is significantly associated with convictions for violence at 18 years.
- One study demonstrated a link between temperament – children seen as more 'difficult', including tantrums – with adult criminal offences.

Studying the links

Another study attempted to find links to younger children. The researchers looked at adult convictions and traced them back to a sample who had been the subject of a large study of behaviour problems in pre-school children.

Key findings
- From the original list of measures, management difficulties, temper tantrums and recent-onset daytime enuresis (wetting) in pre-school children were related to having an adult violent offence.
- The presence of soiling, daytime enuresis, high activity level and management difficulties were related to having any adult conviction.
- The only other factors that could be demonstrated to be linked with later convictions were gender (there was a greater proportion of boys) and the child's social competence at age 3 years.

This gives us a rather depressing picture, but one that is probably all too familiar to many nursery staff, teachers and psychologists, and possibly even parents. It does appear that some children who display difficult behaviour, including bad tantrums, at 3 years old will continue to be a problem right the way through to adulthood.

Above The better a child's social competence, the less likely he is to have behavioural problems in later life.

The importance of parenting

Interestingly, the type of family and their social circumstances could not predict which children might 'go off the rails', demonstrating the importance of parenting skills.

All this offers one good reason why it is especially important for parents to take all the steps they can to work out ways of dealing with difficult behaviour and cutting down on tantrums.

19

understanding
your toddler

2

- Just normal!

- More difficult children

- Are boys harder to handle?

- Children who don't have tantrums

Just normal!

Think back to the story of the Garden of Eden. Adam and Eve had been told that they could eat everything except one forbidden fruit – so what did they do? Of course, they couldn't resist trying out the one thing they had been told not to do!

Above *Allowing your child to brush her own teeth (with supervision) makes her feel more grown up.*

This probably demonstrates an important lesson about the human need to exert self-will and challenge authority, which is at its peak in toddlers. It is part of being human to have your own ideas, thoughts and needs that you want to express and assert.

However, life with some toddlers can resemble a war zone – 'No, no, no', 'I won't', 'Mine', 'Can't make me' – and the battles have a nasty habit of making normally calm, sane adults want to turn into toddlers themselves! It can be an uncomfortable realization for parents that their child is simply determined to get into a battle of wills, and any parent who has been confronted by a toddler determined to win a struggle knows just how hard it can be.

Normal development checklist: 1 to 3 years

A child this age
- resents any form of control
- strives for independence, makes more demands and is more defiant
- swings back and forth between independence and clinginess
- wants control and may try to control his parents, saying to you 'Sit there' or 'Don't touch'
- generally has tantrums.

Inevitably, every toddler from at least 18 months to 3-plus years old, will rebel against your authority and assert his individuality some of the time – that is an absolutely normal part of being a toddler as he constantly tries to explore and learn where the boundaries are.

Your child is almost bound to show some of the range of difficult behaviours, such as being stubborn and defiant (or what psychologists call 'oppositional') as he is developing independence and autonomy. Tantrums are also a normal way of venting feelings that are becoming overwhelming.

When Joe can't get his own way it can cause tantrums, for example about going to bed or having a bath. Another cause is arguing with his older brother, Tom. It usually starts with 'I want Tom's toy.' He can't always get his own way and Tom's toys are not always appropriate for Joe! The tantrums usually consist of shouting, clenching fists and pulling funny faces, but sometimes he resorts to banging his head on the floor, throwing himself on the sofa, and a flood of tears. To get him out of them, the best method is distraction – I might bring him into the kitchen or get out his cars for him to play with.

Sarah, mother of Tom (9) and Joe (2½)

Left *It is normal for a child to have tantrums as he tries to assert his own autonomy.*

More difficult children

If you feel your toddler is harder to handle than most others, there are a number of traits she may display. Looking at these may help you to decide whether or not you have a more difficult child.

Above *Some children are sensitive to their parents' cues while others need direct and repetitious commands.*

Consider the following traits:
- Your child is physically more active than average.
- She is more emotionally intense (for example, she becomes furious if play is stopped).
- She has a more negative outlook (she cries and/or whines more).
- She is more likely to have an irregular schedule (sleeping and eating patterns are often unpredictable).
- She may have a much shorter attention span, and is very easily distracted.
- She finds it much harder to adapt to changes, new people and different situations.

Ask yourself:
- Do I often feel angry and upset with my child?
- Do I often feel she has the upper hand or is taking advantage of me?
- Do I think my child has more, or worse, tantrums than other children?

If the answer to these questions is yes, and she displays many of the traits listed, you may have a more difficult child.

The more strong-willed child often shows extreme forms of the normal behaviours for toddlers – that is, she is even more stubborn, cries more and has more tantrums. It's not easy, but a child like this needs even more calm and patience, extra time to accept changes and loving firmness from her parents.

Born difficult?

There is no doubt that different personality traits can be present from birth. Nine different elements of temperament have been identified in research – such as activity levels, adaptability and mood – which last throughout life and can give a good indication of a child's behaviour.

Babies may show differences in responsiveness right from the start, levels of activity vary greatly, and there can be wide variations in how easily they are comforted. One baby may seem easy-going, rarely crying and sleeping through the night from a few months old; another will have horrendous colic, keep you up at night for years and reject most of your attempts to comfort her.

Similarly, one toddler may be more sensitive and react to very small cues from parents: 'I would like you to pick up your toys' or 'You need to put on your coat, as it's raining' is all that's needed to get the appropriate response. In contrast, another child needs very definite, direct commands before she will react – getting down to her level and saying in a firmer tone of voice 'It's time to pick up your toys now' or 'You must wear your coat today or you will be soaked,' probably repeated several times before it gets through.

If you are finding your toddler hard to handle, it is important to keep in mind that temperament will play some part.

From a young age Lauren has been such a strong-willed child we thought she was possessed by demons! She just knows that she can throw a tantrum to try and get a certain toy she wants. At the shops, if she is told she can't have something she lies down, demanding the toy, knowing she will soon have an audience. However, I try not to give in and move behind a pillar or counter until she stops. Now she is coming up to 3 and I think it's getting worse.

Anne-Marie, mother of Lauren (2½)

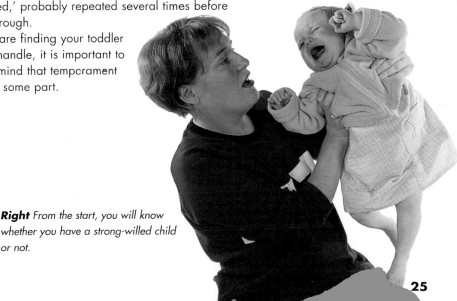

Right From the start, you will know whether you have a strong-willed child or not.

Are boys harder to handle?

It does seem that boys often demonstrate more of the behaviour parents find difficult – what psychologists call 'externalizing' behaviour, which involves 'acting out' and, from your point of view, acting up. Such behaviours include aggression, defiance and over-exuberant physical activity.

Golden Rules

1 Avoid using too many commands or ultimatums.

2 Avoid labels like 'stubborn', 'brat' or 'always has tantrums'.

3 Don't give in to misbehaviour like whining or tantrums once you have said no.

4 Never get angry or aggressive back – this creates a vicious circle.

Left *Children benefit from being brought up in a warm and loving household with clear behavioural boundaries.*

However, this may not all be due to a genuine sex difference. Parents may influence it by their thinking on what is 'masculine' – encouraging more rough play in their sons, for example, or being less accepting of tears as a response to frustration in boys than they are of anger.

A bad match?

When your child's temperament doesn't fit well with yours as a parent, it can be a recipe for trouble. For example, if you are an optimistic, less emotionally intense, more adaptable type of person you may cope easily with difficult behaviour and tantrums in your child, but if you share the more volatile characteristics it can lead to big clashes of will, and you may have to work harder to overcome this.

As your child grows, inborn characteristics of his temperament persist, but they can be shaped and altered by his experiences and your style of parenting. On the positive side, a more stubborn nature and qualities of persistence can be a great attribute in later life, and such adults are often highly successful. But the wrong kind of parenting choices can turn such traits into a life-long problem, if children are allowed to become more and more out of control.

Positive, assertive parenting

It's important for parents to strike the right balance in response to strong-willed defiance: giving in completely almost guarantees ever-worsening behaviour and more tantrums as the child grows up, yet the use of power and force, yelling and smacking always makes the behaviour worse.

A style of parenting that is warm and loving, but at the same time creates a structure and limits, is essential for dealing with the stronger-willed child and keeping tantrums to a minimum.

Above *Both nature and nurture play their part in the more exuberant and aggressive physical activity that boys display.*

27

Children who don't have tantrums

As already mentioned, I do not consider that any of my children had what could be described as full-blown tantrums, even though one baby was an excessive crier who did have a frightening breath-holding episode in her first year. I have since spoken to several parents who insisted their children did not have tantrums.

Her feelings are real

It is important to validate your child's feelings. When you say, 'Stop that silly crying' or 'That doesn't matter, you'll be fine', you are not recognizing how your child feels. It is important to try to accept and understand your child's sadness and fears, and such acceptance gives her a very important message. 'You must be feeling sad to cry like that' or 'That must be making you really mad' shows that you care and understand. It also encourages your child to express feelings in a healthy way, and to talk to you about emotions and worries as she grows older.

Parents' definitions

One explanation may lie in the different ways in which parents define tantrums: some may call a minor crying protest a tantrum, while others think of a tantrum as the lying on the floor, legs kicking, high-pitched screaming, most extreme variety.

All toddlers will inevitably get angry and frustrated sometimes, but not all will throw a complete screaming fit over it. Some who have particularly well-developed language may be able to express their frustration verbally; others may not actually have a tantrum but drive parents mad by going against just about everything they are asked to do. In a few families, the parents may also be desperate to avoid such intense displays of anger and rage, because they are not comfortable themselves with such emotions, and do everything they can to keep them well hidden.

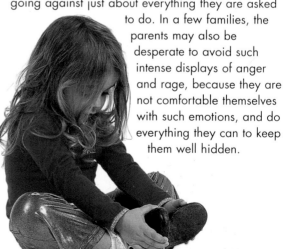

Happy and sad

Parents naturally want their children to be happy. When this is the case, it can feel as if all's right with the world – 'I love you, you're the bestest mummy in the world' just lifts your spirits. It can be really hard to bear when your child turns into a little monster, even if only temporarily. 'I hate you, go away – you're a horrible mummy' can be very hurtful.

However, it is important to accept that your child will feel sad and upset some of the time. Trying to overcome difficulties, getting mad, feeling frustrated, being sad and bursting into tears are all just as much part of life as the happy times, and these are important lessons for toddlers. After all, unless we sometimes feel down, we can't appreciate how great it is to be happy.

Left *It is important to understand that sometimes your child will feel sad and scared.*

Right *Sharing a cuddle with your child is good for you and for her.*

Bailie doesn't really have temper tantrums – she whinges, cries or will have 'jelly legs' and collapse on the floor. It is usually if she is tired or can't get her own way. She will go into a sulk, or if she's tired she will take herself off to bed. Her older sister, Ellie, also never had temper tantrums – she now sulks or gives dirty looks if she doesn't get her own way!

Rebecca, mother of Ellie (6½) and Bailie (3)

My husband Fred just doesn't think the children have tantrums, because they are ready for bed when he comes home! Liam sometimes throws himself on the floor, kicking and screaming, especially if he is tired. I remember when we went to a toddler group and he wanted to grab the other children's toys. Obviously he couldn't have them and it led to a tantrum. I do find holding and hugging him helps.

Fiona, mother of Liam (3) and Nicole (1½)

what causes tantrums?

3

- Tantrum triggers

- Identifying flashpoints

Tantrum triggers

There are some things that can trigger tantrums in almost any child, regardless of their natural character. Unfortunately for parents, the list of possible 'tantrum triggers' is quite long!

Right There are numerous things that can trigger a tantrum, some of which are attention-seeking, wanting what isn't hers, trying to show how independent she is and becoming frustrated or overtired.

You may find your child's tantrums triggered by any of the following:

- **Attention-seeking** A child's first tantrums don't start just to get attention and are rarely done to manipulate parents, but if the reward for a tantrum is massive amounts of satisfactory attention from the adults around him, it can provide a very good reason to have another one again soon! This is why it is particularly important to try not to over-react or make a huge fuss, but to act calmly, even if you don't feel like it.

- **Wanting something he can't have** Whether it's sweets you've said no to or a toy taken from another child, learning to wait for things he wants or accepting that he can't have everything he desires takes a long time.

- **Wanting to prove he's independent** Your child may be desperately trying to show you that he is a separate person with his own views – for example, by demanding to wear a particularly unsuitable item of clothing, such as a T-shirt on a freezing cold day. If you won't let him, even for very good reasons, he may feel that his growing independence is being threatened. It is this deeper fear that makes the reaction seem so out of proportion to parents.

- **Inner frustration** The feeling of growing impatience with his own limited ability to succeed at the things he tries, or not being able to express fully what he wants because of a lack of language skills, can trigger a tantrum. This can start with a determination to do things by himself – 'Me do it' – such as putting on his own clothes or finding the pieces of a puzzle on his own, only to find he gets stuck and in a muddle half-way through. Alternatively, he might want you to pass a toy down from a high shelf or a biscuit from the tin, yet not be able to make you understand. Situations like this lead to anger with himself and the rest of the world.

Dealing with frustration

Keep an eye on your child to make sure that tasks are not too hard and that toys he is playing with are for the right age range. Encourage him to try new challenges, but always be ready to step in before he gets too discouraged: say 'That puzzle must be upsetting you because it's so hard to do – let's find another one.'

- **Jealousy** This is often directed at a brother, sister or another child. Perhaps wanting a toy they have got, or a book they are reading, can set off a tantrum in your child when her desire is not met.
- **Tiredness or hunger** These factors always make it harder to cope with whatever else is happening. Your child generally feels grumpy when she is tired or is in need of a snack, and will then very easily become even crosser at the slightest provocation.
- **Over-stimulation** Sometimes even very enjoyable events like days out, birthday parties or Christmas can be stressful, with the change in familiar routines and the raised emotional temperature. This can lead to tantrums in some children.
- **Emotional overload** A small child will inevitably feel overloaded some of the time with all the new sensations and emotions she experiences, and it is not surprising that she is occasionally overwhelmed by them, so that she seems to fly off the handle. Parents often notice that once the child has let off steam she is more relaxed and cheerful for some time afterwards.
- **'Sheer cussedness'!** Some of the behaviour that ends up leading to tantrums is not easily explained, or at least does not seem to fit perfectly into one category or another. It's the unreasonable 'I want, I won't, me do it' that can drive the most

Left Seeing another child being the centre of attention can easily cause an outburst.

Dealing with 'impossible' situations

The best thing you can do when faced with impossible demands from your child is to try to stay calm and sympathetic. Respect that your child is demonstrating her own confused feelings: say 'You must be feeling sad that you don't have the toy we left behind' or 'You probably really wish you could have the other kind of sweet now – we will buy that one next time.'

reasonable parent to despair. Many say that there are times when their child just seems set on having a tantrum no matter what they do.

You probably know the scenario: your child gives you an impossible task, like demanding a toy that has been left back home once you have driven miles on the way to granny's; or, she changes her mind about the sweet that you just bought her and wants a different one five minutes after you have left the shop.

Above Even a fun day out can end in tears if your child beomes over-tired or over-stimulated.

Identifying flashpoints

Many everyday situations can lead to the build-up of anger or frustration that can turn into a tantrum. It really is worth planning ahead to keep these to a minimum.

Above Your child will be into everything, so make sure that precious belongings are kept well out of reach.

The following pages describe some common flashpoints, and offer strategies for dealing with them.

Wants to be into everything

Your child's natural and overwhelming desire to make exciting discoveries about the world means that he is almost bound to touch the television controls, or try to stick a toy into the video, or tip your handbag into the toilet! He just can't help himself emptying out the contents of drawers – and it never seems as much fun putting things back. He will often be tempted to climb up on anything handy to see what is going on above his own level.

Strategies

1 Accept that you can't change his curiosity, and it would probably be harmful to try. Constantly having to say 'no', and stopping every adventure he starts, is almost bound to lead to tantrums.

2 To keep yourself sane, it makes much more sense to 'toddler-proof' your home as much as possible, moving dangerous or valuable possessions out of reach.

3 Try to keep one step ahead, thinking about the next stage and working out what will tempt your toddler.

Refusing to get into a buggy or car seat

Most toddlers view it as a threat to their independence to be strapped in with their freedom restricted, or to have to ride while everyone else walks.

Strategies

1 If you are not in a rush, let your child walk at least sometimes. If he insists on pushing the buggy and you are worried that it may bash into other people's legs or, more dangerously, tip into the road, try giving your child a small toy version while you hang on to the real one.

2 In the car, there is no room for negotiation. Make it clear that everyone has a 'buckle-up' time before you drive off, and never allow anyone to get away with not doing this. Remaining calm and assertive is the best way to deal with this problem.

3 Distraction techniques can sometimes help to take a child's mind off things long enough for you to get going. These include:
- Chatting non-stop about where you are going and what you will do there.
- Letting him strap in a teddy or doll at the same time.
- Bursting into a funny song, such as 'The wheels on the buggy go round and round' or 'Humpty Dumpty sat in his car seat'.
- Playing a favourite story tape on the journey.

Above *While you know that your child's safety is paramount, all he can see is that you have restricted his freedom.*

37

Above Find time for a trip to the park to allow your child to look around and discover new things without being rushed.

Always wants to dawdle

The whole world is a new and exciting place for toddlers, and there are lots of fascinating things to discover. Your child might spot an insect in a crack or a lovely shiny pebble, and she is likely to think of any trip as a great opportunity to study these, not just as a way of getting from A to B. Trying to force her to rush often leads to a tantrum.

Strategies

1 Try to accept that you need longer for journeys with your toddler, to give her time to check out all the fascinating findings on the way.

2 If you really are in a rush and can't spare the time, use clever tricks to keep things moving: say 'I bet you can't beat me to reach that lamppost,' turning it into a fun race.

3 Provide times in the garden or at the park when she can explore to her heart's content.

Resists being kept clean and tidy

Many toddlers make a fuss when it comes to hygiene, whether this is hair brushing or washing, brushing teeth or taking a bath. On a bad day, being forced to do any of these things can mean that tantrums threaten.

Strategies

1 Let your child have a go at doing these things herself. But be ready to step in if she gets cross when it is not going well.

2 Try providing a doll that your child can clean while you are carrying out the tasks.

3 Distract her with a toy or song while the job is being done.

Asks endless questions

Constantly repeated 'Why?' and 'What's that?' questions can feel irritating to parents and it is tempting to say that you don't know or even to tell your child to shut up, but this can make a toddler very cross and lead to tantrums.

Strategies

Try to consider things from your child's point of view:

1 She wants to learn as much as possible about the world, and you are the best person to help with this.

2 Using newly acquired language and playing the questions-and-answers game is still a bit of a novelty.

3 It is a useful way for her to capture your attention and to find things out at the same time.

4 Do your best not to act too bored with this stage, and to answer as patiently as you can. Remember that you are teaching your child all the time, and providing an invaluable head start for formal education.

Above Expect to be questioned about anything and everything!

Below Try to distract your child with a toy to avert a tantrum.

Doesn't want to share

A toddler thinks of everything as 'mine'. It takes quite a long time for him to learn that some things don't belong to him, or that his possessions can be shared. Forcing him to share before he is ready, or snatching away a toy to give to another child, can lead to horrendous tantrums. Think about how you might feel if you were expected to share your car, jewellery, or other prized possessions!

Strategies

1 Teach the sharing concept gradually and by your example, saying things like 'This is my milk, this is your juice' and 'This is my purse, this is your teddy.'

Above All toddlers think of toys as their own property and being forced to share can easily cause tempers to fray.

2 Don't expect too much with friends or playmates at this age. Many children won't really play co-operatively until they are over 3 years old. It is pointless trying to force a younger toddler to share, because he won't understand what is involved. You can continue to give patient explanations.

3 Allow your child to pack away precious possessions when friends visit, only leaving out toys he is happy to let others play with. He may be more willing to share if he sees that not everything he owns is up for grabs.

Is always interrupting

Your toddler is happiest when he is centre stage with your undivided attention. This can show itself by not letting you chat to friends or speak on the phone. He may interrupt you constantly, even climb up on you, or put a hand over your mouth! In desperation, he may throw a tantrum to guarantee that your attention shifts.

Strategies

1 Keep calls and visits to friends short when your toddler is around.

2 Consider saving your calls for when he's down for a nap.

3 Spend some time sorting him out with something to play with before you start to chat.

4 Explain patiently over and over again what you need to do – but remember that it will be some time before he understands and accepts this.

Just can't wait

Impatience and wanting things now are normal features of every young child's character. Your child can't understand why he can't have a video on immediately, even though you're on the phone; or why a story can't be read straight away, while you are making tea. He wants to be by the seaside even though you have only just started on the long drive – and is likely to say 'Are we there yet?' often.

Strategies

1 It helps to realize that your toddler thinks of himself as the centre of the world, and feels as if his own immediate needs are more important than anything or anybody else.

2 He doesn't really understand the concepts of 'later' or 'in a minute' – you can help by using timers or pointing to where the hands of the clock will be.

3 Gradually work at getting him used to the idea of time and waiting: say 'As soon as I finish the washing up I will help you out with the puzzle' or 'By the time the song finishes on the radio, we will be at nursery.'

Nicole started to get upset when I was on the phone and always wanted to take it from me. I gave her a toy phone of her own which looked identical and it really worked – she has just stopped doing that.

Fiona, mother of Liam (3) and Nicole (1½)

Above *If your child gets upset when you're on the phone, why not get her one of her own so she can copy you?*

41

One time when Amber was younger and we were swimming, I was ready to get out but she didn't want to. She started whining to stay in, then shouting 'I don't want to, I don't want to get out.' I told her calmly that if she didn't get out I would not be able to bring her the next week. This soon stopped her and she got out.

Loretta, mother of Amber (6)

Demands rituals

This is absolutely normal behaviour in many toddlers, but can seem quite strange to adults. Lunch has to be served only on the blue floral plate; a sandwich has to be cut in exact square shapes; old, much loved, but now too small shoes won't be given up; it has to be the same bedtime story over and over again. Trying to force your child to accept changes before she is ready is simply asking for a tantrum.

Strategies

1 Accept that all of these behaviours are an attempt by your toddler to control and make sense of her world.

2 It is much easier to go along with your child and humour her needs until she decides for herself to grow out of them.

3 Your child is the best judge of when she is ready to give up these habits.

Below *Wanting the same story read over and over may be be boring for you, but is normal behaviour for a toddler.*

Constant demands and whining for things she can't have

Parents can be driven to distraction by whining requests. Sometimes it is for something: 'Want an ice-cream' or 'Read the story again'. Sometimes it is a more generalized moaning and bad mood – perhaps made worse by hunger, tiredness or coming down with an illness. Whatever the reason, these whiny episodes have a nasty habit of escalating into tantrums.

Strategies

1 Make sure *you* don't whine when asking your child to do something.

2 The best strategy is a calm refusal to respond to whining.

3 You do have to recognize your child's frustrations, otherwise she will get more and more annoyed. You can't give in to everything your toddler wants, but it can help to explain: say 'I know you feel cross that I won't buy the ice cream, but we are going home for lunch' or 'You can't put a tape on now as it will soon be bedtime.'

4 Think about what might be your child's real need behind the whining. Remember, sometimes 'I want' is really a code for wanting a bit of attention from you – a cuddle, or a bit of praise, or a few minutes spent sitting on your lap, and your child may be happy to go off playing again.

Below *When your child is whining, often all she really wants is a cuddle.*

can tantrums
be avoided?

4

- Avoidance tactics

- Heading off tantrums

- Everyday battlegrounds

Avoidance tactics

Avoiding tantrums may seem an impossible dream, but it really can be done – with a bit of forward planning and some thinking about how your child views the world.

George has never really had a bad tantrum. Some things can be tricky, and we do get tears if he doesn't get his own way. Sometimes he demands chocolate or crisps, and when I say 'no' he decides to cry. I leave him to it and walk out of the room. Most of the time he will stop if I do that. Other times I distract him by giving him a toy or going off to show him something.

Yvette, mother of George (2½)

Below *Always praise behaviour that you want to encourage.*

tips for success

- Try to see things from your child's point of view. It sometimes helps to think back to how you felt as a child, and how unfair the adult world seemed then.

- Have sensible expectations. A great deal of behaviour that parents describe as 'naughty' is just a normal part of development. It can help to confirm this with other parents. You will probably find that all children of a similar age are behaving in similar ways.

- Try to keep family rules to a minimum, so that your child isn't over-whelmed by the amount that he is expected to remember and live up to.

- Have recognizable family routines. If things happen in a certain way or at particular times each day, your child will soon get used to it and this helps to cut down on the need for battles.

- Be realistic. It is normal for your child to test your reaction and to try things over and over, even when you have said no – this is part of his development and of learning what is and isn't acceptable behaviour.

- Teach by example. Children learn most of their behaviour and ways of dealing with situations by copying adults. If you don't want your child to behave aggressively or to fly into tantrums, then it's important that you don't either.

- Always make allowances for a child who is overtired or ill, when behaviour is usually worse for a while.

- Give him plenty of opportunities for exercise. Providing lots of time to run around, enjoy active play or dance to music tapes can help to avoid frustrations.

- Offer plenty of praise whenever your child is behaving well and quietly.

- Keep a sense of humour! The more that parents can manage to stay positive and try to see the humorous side of annoying behaviour, the happier everyone will be.

Heading off tantrums

Sometimes there is a moment when a threatening tantrum can be headed off, if you spot the danger in time and then act quickly enough to defuse the situation.

Below Sometimes it is possible to head off a tantrum before it really gets going.

There are a number of elements to recognizing and dealing with situations that may lead to tantrums.

Early warning signs

Keep an eye on your child's behaviour, so that you are alert to any signals that she is becoming frustrated.

- Is she trying to fit a piece into a puzzle that is just too difficult and becoming furious that the piece won't fit?
- Is she getting stuck with a jumper half-way on?
- Has she been trying to get your attention for some time while you were talking to a friend?

You need to step in to help in order to defuse these situations before they reach the tantrum stage.

Avoiding difficult situations

This is another possible strategy in certain circumstances. For example:

- Your daughter hates to be forced to sit in her pushchair inside shops. She may want to see what is going on, or to feel that she is a 'big girl'. Can you allow more time to let her hold your hand and walk? If not, can you possibly shop without her, perhaps taking turns with a partner or friend?

Saying no

If you want your toddler to be less negative, use phrases like 'You can have it later' instead of 'No, you can't have it', or 'Playing with the bricks would be a good idea – you can do it as soon as you get up tomorrow' instead of 'You can't play with it, it is bedtime now.'

Providing a good example

Think about how you behave and the example it provides. If your child sees adults flying into a rage or screaming with frustration at minor upsets, it is much harder for her to learn self-control.

A child needs to see that adults can handle frustration and disappointments without falling apart – this is how she learns to deal with them. If you get angry over a lost parking space or start screaming about a broken fingernail, then you can't expect your child to behave calmly when she has to deal with the inevitable stresses of everyday life.

Giving her some control

It is very hard for a small child to feel she never has a say. She sees that adults have all the power and make all the decisions – where to go, what to do and what to buy. Let her have choices whenever you can, over what to wear or eat, or what to play with. Say 'Do you fancy fish fingers or beans on toast for tea?' or 'Shall we get out your bricks or your cars?'

Below You can try and divert or distract your child with his favourite toy or book.

Advance warnings

Give your child time and warnings before moving on to new activities: say 'Your bath will be ready in five minutes' or 'In ten minutes we will need to put the toys away to go to nursery'. A timer can help him to understand this.

Distraction

- **Diversion** Even if you think a tantrum is starting to brew up, there is often time to divert your child. Quickly introducing a new toy, or pointing out something that is happening outside the window – 'Let's see if we can find the red brick' or 'I think I hear a bus coming – can you hear it?' – can work well, especially with younger children, though by 3 years or so they may have learned to see through this and cannot be fooled as easily.
  - **Substitution** If you quickly offer a toy, your child will happily give up the keys you need. Other examples include offering paper when he tries to draw on the walls, or an old magazine to tear up when he attempts it on your newspaper.

When Eleanor starts, she throws herself on the floor and screams and kicks. I try distracting her by singing a nursery rhyme or suggesting we watch her favourite television programme. She also loves looking at any photographs and playing with the frame, so I sometimes get her one down.

Gabriella, mother of Eleanor (1½)

Spotting a pattern

If your child has a lot of tantrums, it can help to keep a written record of exactly what is happening beforehand, and what the circumstances are at the time a tantrum starts. For example:

- Is it often while you are making lunch? Try letting him help you set the table, or organize him near you with an interesting toy or game before you start to prepare the meal.
- Is it usually at night, when you come home tired from work? Perhaps it would help if he could have a bath supervised by your partner while you unwind.

Right If your child seems to have more tantrums than usual, try to keep a written record to see if there is a trigger for it, such as tiredness.

51

Everyday battlegrounds

There are a number of situations that arise every day that can turn into battlegrounds and result in repeated tantrums over the same issues. Taking time to work out how to avoid these is well worth the effort!

Right On days when it doesn't matter what your child wears, let her make her own choice.

tips for success

- Try letting your child make her own choice of outfits and as many decisions as possible for herself. Make your life easier by only offering choices that are suitable for the weather and occasion, and keeping others well out of sight.

- If you have to say no to her choice, explain your reasons. Perhaps she wants to wear pyjamas to go to a friend's party – explain that there are times when we need to dress up nicely, so that she understands there is a reason, and that you are not simply saying no to annoy her.

- Accept that your toddler wants comfort and something that appeals to her – nothing else about clothes is of any significance.

- Think about whether you might be too invested in what other people think, so that you feel judged as a parent if someone considers an outfit foolish. Often parents' own self-esteem is tied into dressing up a child.

- Vow not to get into power struggles: most children then do the exact opposite to show their own preferences. Be laid back and say 'That's an interesting outfit you picked out,' while gritting your teeth over the orange polka dot shorts and purple T-shirt!

- If there can be no choice, be firm but kind about this. For example, if it is pouring with rain so that she has to wear a coat, say 'We do have to put your coat on today or you will be soaked through,' so that she learns that sometimes parents have to make the decisions.

The tips provided here should help you to look at these situations with a fresh eye and devise successful strategies for coping with them.

'I'll wear what I want.'

It's a cold, wet morning, but your toddler is digging in her heels: 'I want to wear my yellow shorts.' Remember that small children just choose what they like or whatever attracts their attention first, not something sensible. As soon as she can begin choosing her own clothes then the battles may start.

This is one area where parents could often save themselves a lot of heartache and upset. Ask yourself whether it really matters what your child wears on a particular occasion – maybe there are times when you could be more flexible.

'Don't want to eat it.'

Food is another battleground that is best avoided with a strong-willed child. Your toddler knows when he feels full. If are you determined to make him eat it all up, stop to think how you might feel if the waiter in a restaurant insisted you couldn't leave until you had eaten everything on your plate! If he absolutely refuses to eat it or starts threatening a tantrum, calmly take it away and say 'You're obviously not hungry now.'

Tips for success

- Don't make a big fuss over mealtimes – let your toddler have as much control and choice as possible.
- Limit choices by saying 'Would you like pasta or pizza for dinner?' or 'Do you want cereal or porridge for breakfast?' This helps to avoid jelly and ice cream and sweets at every meal!
- Let your child have the absolute right to say when he has had enough.

Below If there isn't time for her to put her own shoes on, acknowledge her frustration and set aside some time later for her to practise when you aren't rushed.

- When he begins playing with food or throwing it around, take it away and say calmly 'All finished now.'
- Have clear, simple rules and stick to them, for example: 'We only eat at the table, not wandering around the room' or 'Once you leave the table, there is no more food until teatime.' Then don't give in when he says he's hungry five minutes after you clear away. This may cause upset, but remind him calmly 'What a pity you didn't feel hungry at lunchtime.'

'Me want to do it.'

There are only five minutes to go before you need to have your toddler out of the door, but he won't let you help to put on his shoes: 'I'm a big boy – me do it.' This is one of those times when you may have to be firm about doing it for him.

Tips for success

- Allow a few minutes for your child to try, even when you have to be somewhere: say 'You try first, but after five minutes I have to help you or I will be late.' Be firm but kind when the time is up.
- Acknowledge the angry feelings that are inevitably stirred up when you have to take over: 'I know you want to do it yourself, but we don't have time now – we can try again next time.'
- Expect anger from a child who has been thwarted in a desire to be independent, but be calm yourself: say 'I know it makes you mad, but you can practise later.'
- At less pressured times, provide lots of opportunities for him to practise skills and give lots of praise for his efforts.

dealing
with tantrums

5

- Handling minor tantrums

- Dealing with public tantrums

- Dealing with major tantrums

Handling minor tantrums

You can sometimes judge from the trigger situation whether it is one that is likely to lead to a tantrum in which your child will not become totally out of control. These episodes often start with whining for something, then develop into a tantrum.

It's important that you don't say no to begin with and then give in to demands at this later stage, or your child will quickly learn that if she carries on for long enough, you can be worn down. If you are going to give in to a demand, do it right at the beginning before a tantrum starts.

Below *Trying to ignore minor outbursts can sometimes work to defuse the situation.*

Tips for success

- Give reasons. If, for example, your child whines for ice cream on the way home from nursery and you don't want her appetite spoiled for lunch, try saying kindly but firmly 'There's no point in making that fuss. We will soon be having lunch, so I can't let you spoil your appetite now with ice cream' – then refuse to be drawn into any further discussions on the topic.
- Be calm and consistent. On occasions when it has to be 'no', don't get caught up in emotional battles. Repeat your position calmly: 'I said no sweets now, because it will soon be dinner time.'
- Use the 'broken record' approach, repeating a statement calmly several times but not being trapped into further arguments.

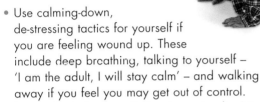

- Use calming-down, de-stressing tactics for yourself if you are feeling wound up. These include deep breathing, talking to yourself – 'I am the adult, I will stay calm' – and walking away if you feel you may get out of control.
- Ignore the behaviour. Trying (or pretending) to ignore minor tantrums sometimes works – simply carry on with whatever you were doing or walk off into another room. This can be successful for all minor misbehaviours.
- It can make some children even more angry to be ignored completely, so you could say something like 'I'm not taking any notice until you ask properly and stop that whining,' then walk away from the manipulative crying. If you find this particularly difficult, try reading a magazine or starting up the hoover.
- There should be a clear time limit on ignoring – no more than five minutes is appropriate for younger children. If the tantrum has not ended, try saying 'Right, it is time to stop now – by the time I count to ten,' and give lots of praise and hugs if your child manages to get herself back under control.
- Expect good behaviour. Saying something like 'I'd like you to play quietly while I am talking on the phone' or 'It would be great if you could help me while we are shopping' can sometimes encourage the response you want.

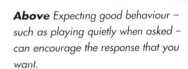

Above *Expecting good behaviour – such as playing quietly when asked – can encourage the response that you want.*

Being told she can't have something can start Natasha off – she throws herself on the floor and kicks her feet – but she just comes round on her own if you ignore it and leave her for a few minutes.

Mark, father of Natasha (2)

Dealing with public tantrums

Tantrums that occur when you are out and about are often the hardest to cope with. In the supermarket other shoppers are looking on, tutting disapprovingly, and when you are visiting others it can feel horribly embarrassing. To avoid such scenes, it helps to plan ahead!

Out shopping

These are the worst possible tantrums for many parents. If at all possible, it can make life easier if you shop without your toddler, unless he has to be there for something like new shoes. Think about whether a partner or friend could help to look after him.

If you have to take your toddler shopping at the supermarket:
• Plan ahead almost as you would to go on a trip. Take along snacks, drinks and toys, then try giving your child a snack or drink as soon as you enter the shop.
  • Keep trips as short as possible. Make lists so that you know exactly what you are there to buy.
    • When you have time, let your child help you by passing things from the shelf into the trolley – this can work wonders with a child who feels really useful finding you the kitchen roll or cereal.

Left *If you take your young child shopping, plan ahead and, if you have time, let her help you out.*

When Amber was around 3 years old, in the supermarket she would whine for crisps or sweets, and if I said no she just sat on the floor and cried and screamed. I left her there and moved away where I could still see her, but she couldn't see me. When she realized I wasn't there she soon calmed down. I then came back to explain that crying and screaming doesn't get you what you want.

Loretta, mother of Amber (6)

- Have an interesting toy for your child to play with while you are going round – the musical wind-up ones that attach to the pushchair or trolley can't be thrown away in a temper and often work well to amuse.
- Chat constantly about what you are doing. Say, for example, 'I am choosing the coffee now' and 'I am just checking which are the best apples.'
- Make a game of things whenever you can. Sing a silly nursery rhyme, or play at seeing who can spot the cereal first.
- With older toddlers, talk before you go about how you want them to behave, and agree in advance whether you will be buying sweets.
- Decide whether the corner shop would do and avoid the supermarket!

If, in spite of all your efforts, a tantrum does start it is probably better to pick up your child, get out of the shop as quickly as possible and try again later. Even if you have to leave your shopping behind, there is little point in creating a scene and ending up upset and embarrassed.

Above Visiting friends is good for you and your child, but remember that your child may play up if she is not the centre of attention.

Visiting friends

Toddlers are generally happiest when they are the centre of attention. This means that they may tend to play up more when your attention is directed away from them and towards friends. Try the following strategies:

- Keep trips as short as possible if you know your child is likely to become bored.
- Keep an eye on her frustration level. Pay attention to any signals she is giving that she is becoming annoyed. Don't become so engrossed in chatting that you let things escalate until it is too late.
- Try not to be so embarrassed in front of others that you act quite differently from how you would at home – demanding standards like sitting up at the table, for example – as your child will easily spot this and play up.
- If you are going out to somewhere which is not 100 per cent 'child-friendly', it is worth taking along a small bag full of toys and treats so that your child will remain busy or so that any signs of an upcoming tantrum can perhaps be diverted by a small 'surprise'. This should be used rarely so that your child does not behave well only when there is a reward.
- Remember to give lots of praise whenever your child behaves well in these tricky situations: say something like 'You must have felt bored and yet you still behaved really well.'

Dealing with major tantrums

Sometimes your child's feelings seem to get more and more out of control, and you know that there is no way he is going to let you divert him out of it. In a major tantrum, your child really cannot control his feelings or listen to any reason, and he is also likely to be frightened himself by the overwhelming nature of the episode.

> Holding or hugging a child tightly can be harder than it sounds! David is so big and heavy already that I can't just easily pick him up for a hug, or to take him out of a shop.
>
> *Jane, mother of David (3)*

The advice to try to ignore the behaviour, as you might do with less dramatic tantrums, won't work well now, as your child will probably become even more scared if you do this. He needs to know that you are still in control even when he has lost it.

Tips for success

- For the youngest toddlers, up to about 2 years old, actions always speak louder than words. Reasoning probably won't work: instead, lift him away from the video or into a safe place like a cot or pushchair; distract him away from the cat food with a biscuit. You can also hug him tightly when a tantrum threatens.
- Do everything you can to stay calm yourself. Breathe deeply, count to ten, tune out whining, pause before you act – try not to let your child 'press your buttons'.
- Speaking calmly to your child in a quiet voice, letting him know that you won't punish or leave him, sometimes makes him stop to listen – or at least helps to take the noise down to a bearable level!
- Holding your child firmly in a tight hug sometimes works, but probably only if you can remain calm, and it can make a few children even more angry. A small child who is totally out of control has to be prevented from hurting himself or others. This

may mean holding him tightly or moving things out of his path. Stress that you are just trying to stop him hurting himself or you. If he won't let you hold him and it is making him even more mad, stay close by until the storm is over.

Martha Welch's book *Holding Time* advises:
- making direct eye contact
- talking quietly
- continuing to hold tightly.

She says that the child may seem to protest more, struggle violently and become more angry to begin with, but that this will generally subside into a relaxed phase and cuddling if you persevere.

Right *Holding your child tightly stops him from hurting himself if he totally loses control.*

The one thing that causes Kieron to freak out and have a complete meltdown is an argument over who is going to open the garage door, then who is going to be first to open the car door. Tammy and I find the best way to deal with this is time out. We try to be consistent and follow through once we have insisted on something. We do use 'time-outs' – leaving him to sit quietly for about a minute in the house or car (where we can see him). He usually calms down in about 30 seconds.

Clem and Tammy, parents of Megan (5) and Kieron (3)

Time-out

- If your own feelings of anger are threatening to become too strong and you feel that you are in danger of losing control, it may be safer to walk into another room and take some cooling-down time for yourself. Tell your child that this is what you are doing, and that you will come back soon to look after her. This is better than losing your temper, shouting and making an already bad situation worse.
- When you do feel calm, talk to your child. Say 'You must be feeling very mad and upset. That's OK, but I won't let you hit or kick' – sometimes you may have to hold a child to prevent this as she will automatically lash out. You are teaching your child a very important lesson: angry feelings can be managed, and that you are still in control and won't let anything awful happen to her.
- Take time-out. This involves putting your child in another room or designated place until she calms down. However, it is not always practical for very young children, who can't or won't co-operate with the idea. If the child has to be forced, it is likely to inflame her anger more and will only make the situation worse.
- Time-out works best for the over-threes. It is a useful alternative for some parents for any misbehaviour that you cannot ignore, such as fighting or being destructive – it is impossible to ignore a child ripping off the wallpaper or snatching another child's toy!
- When a tantrum is over, don't keep on nagging or reminding your child about it. Children often feel very vulnerable afterwards. Cuddle, kiss and make up.

Above *Time-out can work well for older children.*

time-out tips

- Putting your child somewhere boring like a pushchair or playpen, or on the bottom step of the stairs, for a few minutes is the way to do this.

- It should never be forced physically or done in anger, and may not work with very young children.

- Time-out must always be backed up by other parenting methods like praise, love and support.

- Use it positively: say 'Please take time out to cool down and feel better. I'll talk to you when you're calm again,' not 'Right, that's it, you're going to your room and you're not coming out till you learn to behave.'

- Parents can also take personal time-out – use it to give yourself space and to cool down. Take deep breaths, count to ten, take a walk around the garden or go into another room (always make sure your child is safe first).

the positive
approach

6

- Positive parenting

- Positive discipline

- Making humour work for you

Positive parenting

'Positive parents' are warm, nurturing, supportive but reasonably controlling, set high expectations for their children and meet all their needs.

So what do children need from their parents?

A child's needs

- **Love** – this is the most important of all. If you can love your child unconditionally, he will grow up feeling more confident and positive about himself.
- **Attention** – children thrive on lots of positive attention.
- **Praise** – not just for achievements, but for trying things, too. Specific praise, describing exactly what it is given for, works best.
- **Respect** – your child deserves to be treated with the same courtesy you would give another adult.
- **Talking and listening** – these are vital skills for all parents who want to avoid tantrums.
- **Gradual independence** – helping your child learn to do things for himself as soon as he is able to manage will boost his confidence. Encourage him to explore and take on new challenges when you think he is ready for them.
- **Consistency** – this is crucial. It is very confusing for your child if you come down hard on a behaviour one day and then let it go the next.

Above *Love, attention and respect are some of the most important things that you can give your child.*

Parenting styles and tantrums
Authoritarian parenting involves:

- having strict rules, giving orders and using a lot of demands or threats
- using harsh, often physical punishments
- feeling it is a constant battle raising children, and that you must win
- making all the decisions, and overriding your child's wishes or views.

Children raised this way

- may learn to use physical violence or other hurtful methods to solve conflicts
- can be withdrawn, fearful and stressed or, alternatively, angry, hostile and rebellious
- may have more tantrums.

Above Praise your child as he becomes more independent and tries dressing and undressing himself.

Ask the expert

The focus has switched in many families so that many children are completely over-indulged, with parents almost acting like a slave to the child. This may lead to less tantrums, but I think it is bad for children in other ways. It leads to a lack of self-sufficiency – they can't problem solve or think for themselves, and they are not responsible for their own behaviour. They often grow up blaming others for everything that happens to them.

Norma Angeli, health visitor who runs parenting programmes and works with handicapped and disabled children

Permissive parenting involves

- always giving in when your child whines or demands something
- doing everything for your child, almost like a servant, and not expecting her to become independent appropriate to age
- turning a blind eye to all naughty behaviour, even when it is far from minor
- allowing your child to win all power battles, so you lose out on your own needs.

Children raised this way

- grow up believing that their needs are more important than anybody else's and they can do exactly as they please
- may test limits and challenge authority in a more and more desperate attempt to find the control they lack
- are quite likely to use tantrums to get what they want.

Right Try not to always give in to your child's demands.

The ideal to aim for is:

Assertive/democratic parenting (positive parenting)

This is the balanced middle way. It respects children's needs and views, yet parents set firm limits where appropriate and don't forget about meeting their own needs.

Positive parenting involves
- explaining why certain rules are necessary for us all to live happily together, and stating them clearly
- showing your disapproval of a child's misbehaviour, but never using harsh punishments
- giving children choices, within limits, and appropriate to age and stage of development
- using encouragement and praise to gain children's co-operation. This means describing what praise is being given for: 'That was really kind of you, sharing your bricks' or 'Thank you for putting away your toys without being asked,' rather than phrases like 'good boy' or 'good girl'. Increase the praise for more challenging children, giving it for every little bit of effort.

Above Positive parenting helps a child to become a happy and well-balanced individual.

Children raised this way
- are well balanced and happy
- adapt easily to changes
- co-operate well with adults and behave respectfully.
- handle problem solving well and try to succeed
- are much less likely to have tantrums.

Positive discipline

Positive discipline means working at good communication and listening to your child's views, but not being afraid to set clear limits and boundaries to behaviour.

Above Reward your child when she behaves responsibly and does what you ask.

There are a number of techniques you can use to encourage good behaviour in your child and help cut down on tantrums.

Top five strategies

1 Socialization
Even with babies, right from the start you should show loving responsiveness and a gradual setting of routines. As they grow, you need to teach right from wrong, explaining the rules of behaviour and the importance of respecting others' needs and views.

2 Setting boundaries
A child knows deep down that setting limits shows that his parents care. He gradually understands that the boundaries are for his safety and well-being, and may regard too much permissiveness as indifference. No small child can feel secure if he is allowed to do exactly as he pleases. He will often behave more and more badly to find out where the limits are.

Remember: all children test limits. This is completely normal behaviour, especially for younger children. Although it is irritating for parents, it is a necessary part of becoming independent. All children fail to do what parents ask some of the time.

- Remember that limits need to be fair.
- Make any rules reasonable and appropriate to your child's age.
- Give clear, positive and polite but assertive

instructions – showing that you expect your child to do what you ask.

3 Natural consequences

This means allowing your child to experience the consequences that would result from his behaviour if you did not intervene. If he doesn't eat, he will feel hungry; if he doesn't wear a coat, he will feel cold; if he doesn't put away his toys, he can't find them next time.

4 Rewards

These are sometimes needed as extra motivation for a while for very difficult behaviour. They can be whatever your child would most appreciate – an outing, a new toy, a video to watch. **Remember:** hugs and kisses are always great rewards. Star charts are useful in some cases – they can be completed for each period of co-operation, working up to the reward. For example, you give a star for every two hours that he doesn't have a tantrum and stick it on the chart. After a whole day without tantrums, you give the reward. The rewards should gradually be replaced with praise and positive attention as behaviour improves. You need to avoid creating a situation where your child will only do something in order to gain a reward.

5 Natural authority

This involves using your voice and body language assertively, showing that you mean what you say. There is no such thing as a child who 'won't take no for an answer'. A child who behaves like this is testing where the limits are. When you really mean it, your child always takes notice: think of how you would speak or act to stop him running into the road or touching a hot cooker.

Discipline versus punishment

'Discipline' is NOT the same as 'punishment'.

- Discipline involves teaching and guiding your child to behave in ways that fit in with your family's rules, and are generally socially acceptable. There is no 'right way' that works all the time and for every situation.

- Punishment, such as smacking, is not an effective way of getting children to behave well in the long term. Research has shown that it always makes tantrums worse. A punishment may appear to stop undesirable behaviour in its tracks at the time, but it certainly doesn't prevent it in the future.

How positive discipline works

Positive discipline works by making sure your child wants to please you and to keep the good relationship you have built. When you develop trust and a willingness to co-operate in your child, you will both be on the same side concerning discipline.

Above *Praise your child when she has done something that you know is difficult for her, such as sharing her favourite biscuit.*

Your personality and the temperament of your child will influence the methods that work. A quiet, easy-to-manage child may need only very gentle reminders for discipline. A naturally more challenging child may need more hard work from you to encourage her to behave well.

You encourage the behaviour you want by:
- Trying to look for ways in which your child behaves well.
- Giving most attention and praise to behaviour you want your child to repeat whenever possible.
- Turning a blind eye to minor annoying behaviour.
- Saving your 'no's' and battles for the times when there is no choice, such as when her safety is involved.

Negative discipline

Very negative discipline – always expecting your child to be naughty and coming down hard on every small act of misbehaviour – can lead to a lot of conflict in the family and make your child tense and unhappy. It can actually make some children more defiant and more likely to have tantrums.

Also, if parents are determined to show 'who is boss', continually trying to control their child's behaviour and forcing her to do as she is told, they can never relax and just enjoy the fun aspects of parenting.

Be realistic

Working at positive discipline takes a lot of energy and no parent can get it right all the time. There will be days when you are too tired or too busy, and feel that you can't be patient or put in the effort required.

All parents behave in ways they regret, some of the time – scolding or smacking a child or getting close to a tantrum themselves. If this happens, say you are sorry, kiss and make up, and try again. This teaches children to do the same.

Above Remember that a child is naturally exuberant and, if you can, try to ignore minor bad behaviour.

Making humour work for you

One of the great things about life with small children is how easy it is to have fun, and how often there are opportunities for laughter. Using humour as much as possible – making a joke or trying to see the funny side of a situation – can often avoid battles and confrontations.

Charlie Chaplin once said:

" A day without laughter is a day wasted "

Laughter is good news all round. It has been clearly shown in research to be good for the whole family. It lowers blood pressure, reduces stress, raises your spirits when you feel down and releases feel-good 'happy hormones' called endorphins. Even smiling when you are not feeling particularly cheerful has been shown to fool your body into releasing these, so that you actually end up feeling better!

Bringing humour into discipline

Laughter can work especially well for toddler discipline, defusing tricky situations, and avoiding battles where everybody loses and feels bad. It often helps to laugh at yourself as an adult – when you are rigidly insisting on a particular behaviour from your toddler, you are probably taking yourself too seriously.

Some of the more irritating toddler behaviours that adults call 'naughty' usually have a humorous side – if you can let yourself see it! It may not seem that funny at the time when your toddler dumps a bowl of cereal over his head, but think of the many similar incidents in slapstick comedy films that have audiences splitting their sides.

Even the dreaded tantrums can be diverted by a bit of humour at the right time. One mum said she carried a sign saying 'Tantrum in progress' to hold up at the appropriate moment – passers-by would smile or laugh, and her daughter would often forget the tantrum. Another mum said she would lie down and join in her child's tantrum before it really got going – though only at home of course!

Left Use every opportunity to have fun with your child.

Using humour to avoid tantrums

Laughter can often turn the tide against a negative toddler reaction and prevent a tantrum.

- Your toddler completely refuses to put on her shoes and coat, even though it is pouring with rain outside and she will get soaked: say 'Well, I will just have to wear them instead, and be nice and dry,' then make a big performance of forcing your feet into the shoes and arms into the coat, saying something like 'I might need some shrinking powder to get me into these, but I will do it.'
- Your child makes a fuss when you want her to be strapped into the car seat: say 'OK, daddy will sit there instead, and you will have to drive,' then pretend you are trying to climb in. You could add 'Oh dear, I forgot you can't drive and I think daddy is too big for this seat – who could fit into it instead?'
- Pretending your child's favourite Disney character or toy wants her to do something can sometimes make it easier to persuade her: say 'Donald Duck wants you to get in the bath now, or he is going to take it instead, because ducks love the water!'
- Using a funny song for requests often helps to amuse your toddler for long enough for her to go along with it: sing 'Mary, Mary quite contrary how does this seat strap go' as you're strapping her in, or 'This is the way we brush our teeth' as you quickly get the job done.
- Pretending you are going to eat something you want your toddler to have can be effective: saying 'It's my pasta, I want to eat it, it's mummy's favourite' works much better than insisting she eats up.

Right *Tickling your toddler can make her giggle and quickly change her mood.*

Below *Try to persuade your child to do something that she doesn't want to do by singing her a funny song.*

- Imaginary games often work well. If your toddler won't put on her sandals, instead of forcing them on and creating a huge fuss, try pretending you are the 'shoe shop lady'. Ask her to choose between some pairs lined up, saying 'Which pair would you like to buy?'
- Try using humorous games to avoid confrontation. You want your toddler to tidy up some toys: try saying 'I bet you can't put more away than me – let's race.' It's important always to let your toddler win for this to be fun.

Antics like these bring out the giggles in many toddlers, and can turn a mood that is about to develop into a tantrum into something more sunny. Also, remember that laughter is infectious. It is harder to remain in a miserable mood when others are laughing cheerfully!

top five tips

1 Tickling: but always gently, and not if she doesn't like it or is already too cross – always stop when she tells you to.

2 Deliberately changing the words of familiar songs or rhymes: 'Twinkle, twinkle little moon... oops, sorry, what should that be again?' or 'Incy wincy butterfly climbed up the water spout – Oh, silly daddy, you will have to help with this song.'

3 Games that end in a predictable tickle or hug: 'Round and round the garden, like a teddy bear, one step, two step, tickly under there' or 'This little piggy went wee, wee, wee, all the way home.'

4 Putting on a silly voice: squeaky like a mouse or droning like an aeroplane, or pretending to be Donald Duck.

5 Combining songs with silly actions: '1, 2, 3, 4, 5, once I caught a fish alive' – 'catching' your toddler in a hug; '6, 7, 8, 9, 10, then I let her go again' – letting go as you say it; or 'Humpty Dumpty had a great fall' as daddy falls off the chair.

action plan

7

- Helping your child to mature beyond tantrums

- Not happy with your response?

- Helping yourself

- Top ten ways to deal with tantrums

Helping your child to mature beyond tantrums

With 3- to 5-year-olds, it gradually becomes possible to work out strategies together so that tantrums can be avoided. A child this age has greater use of language, and is more able to understand the viewpoint of others.

There are a number of ways in which you can help your child to become more mature in dealing with his feelings:

- Teach your child to use proper words to get what he wants, not crying or whining.
- Teach him how to verbalize anger: 'I felt mad when Tom took my toy.'
- Reflect feelings back: say 'Yes, that must have felt very upsetting.'
- Teach him ways to deal with angry feelings. Practise saying 'I'm angry' and explain that 'We don't scream or hit in our family to get what we want.'
- Help with activities to motivate your child to co-operate. For example, say 'I'll put in the cars if you put away the figures.'
- Teach calming-down strategies. These might include, colouring with crayons, listening to a story tape or running around outside.

Your child can use these to help himself calm down.

- Teach relaxation exercises developed especially for young children:

  1 Flopping like a 'rag doll', allowing arms and legs to go limp.

  2 Blowing out imaginary birthday candles – a deep breath, blowing hard and making a wish.

  3 Tensing then relaxing muscles (remember your antenatal classes to show them how!).

More than just a normal tantrum?

Although it is rare, there may be occasions when a physical cause or underlying health problem exists to make tantrums worse. Examples might be:

- A problem with vision or hearing.
- A chronic illness like asthma.
- A learning difficulty.
- A speech delay.
- Attention deficit hyperactivity disorder (ADHD).
- Autism.

Sometimes the problem is not as obvious, but parents feel the tantrums are out of the ordinary and are completely spoiling the relationship they have with their child.

Check with your health visitor, doctor or local child-health clinic if you are ever really worried – if, for example, your child often hurts himself or others, or is very destructive, or tantrums are becoming more frequent, more intense, or lasting longer.

They can have horrendous tantrums, because their frustrations are so much greater – this can be very hard for parents.

Norma Angeli, health visitor who runs parenting programmes and works with handicapped and disabled children

Below *Try to teach your child to verbalize angry feelings rather than resorting to tantrums.*

Not happy with your response?

If you are unhappy with your response to your child's tantrums, first remember that she is not doing any of it on purpose to annoy you and is not yet aware of your needs.

Below Ask your friends and family for their advice and support.

Ask the experts

I can honestly say I have seen more parents throwing tantrums than I have children. I also think the guilt of work and feeling they don't spend enough time with children may lead to parents indulging them more and giving in to tantrums. It probably also feels like an easier situation day to day for parents, not having to deal with confrontations.

When parents attend courses on managing children's behaviour, tantrums definitely cease to be as much of a problem. The STEPS programme we run is based on quite a firm approach in parenting, giving as much responsibility as possible to children for their own behaviour. It helps parents to get back in charge – I suppose it is really like a management course!

Norma Angeli, health visitor who runs parenting programmes and works with handicapped and disabled children

Think about your own anger and what makes it worse. Do you:

- Feel your child challenges your authority?
- Feel foolish, as if your skills as a parent are being judged in front of others?
- Get cross if you are prevented from carrying on with what you wanted to do?

Trying to work out what is going on can help you to understand your own reactions, so that you can deal with your child's behaviour in a calm, clear-headed way.

If you feel that you are not dealing well with your child's tantrums, this may be a time to seek help. Think about what is happening. Do you:

- Feel unhappy with the way you are handling them?
- Keep giving in to tantrums?
- Feel you are losing it and getting into a rage yourself?

Sometimes friends and family can help out with some support or good advice. Your health visitor or doctor is also often a good place to start, or you could think about joining a parenting course, or perhaps telephoning a helpline.

We do a lot on managing behaviour and tantrums, based on the Family Caring Trust materials. I am always amazed at how well most mothers cope – some are on very deprived estates and are very young and vulnerable, yet they still do a great job.

We talk about not rewarding misbehaviour, giving positive attention, setting boundaries. I always stress that the behaviour that is ignored eventually decreases.

We also have an emphasis on parents sharing ideas and providing strategies themselves – and we stress that if what you are doing now isn't working, it can't do any harm to try something different.

Maggie Fisher, health visitor who runs courses for parents of children up to 6 years old

Helping yourself

As well as trying to find ways for your toddler to have fewer tantrums, it is important to look after yourself. If you can prevent yourself becoming too stressed or worn out, this will make it easier to handle any behaviour problems in your child, and more likely that you will be able to keep up your positive parenting.

Above Allow yourself time to relax and unwind.

It can be enormously wearing looking after a child who is having a lot of tantrums. Even when you manage to divert him, it is a stressful and anxious time, requiring a lot of patience, energy and commitment from you.

It is almost impossible to do this day after day without snapping, unless you take care of yourself. If at all possible, take a regular break from childcare, so that you can do something you enjoy just for yourself.

Tips for survival

- Try to eat a healthy balanced diet, with plenty of fruit and vegetables, do all you can to get enough sleep and take some exercise – all these build up your energy.
- Accept all offers of help with your toddler. A few hours on your own to go and have your hair cut or go to the gym can make all the difference to how you feel.
- Find ways to relax. Choose whatever works best for you: a good book, music, a shopping expedition or meeting friends.
- Make sure you have some couple time with your partner, to talk about the stresses of the day or to enjoy an occasional child-free outing.
- Make the most of the happy times you have with your toddler.

- Use stress-busting strategies:
  1 Deep, calm breathing.
  2 Relaxation exercises.
  3 Meditation.
  4 Watching nature.
- Find great ways to nurture yourself:
  1 Massage.
  2 Planning ahead for enjoyable events.
  3 Doing something creative.
  4 Giving yourself treats.

Be positive

In addition, you need to try to have a positive
outlook on the situation:

- Decide what matters to you and what is really
  important, such as health and safety, and stick to
  firm rules for these – don't pick battles over minor
  struggles such as food or clothes.
- Always think about what is developmentally
  appropriate and normal. Try to accept that
  your child will soon grow out of some difficult
  behaviours anyway when this stage is over –
  there is no point in getting too upset about these.
- Give your child lots of positive feedback such as
  smiles, strokes, hugs and thanks for good
  behaviour you want to encourage, and pat
  yourself on the back when you have a good day.
- Work at creating a support system of relatives,
  friends and neighbours, keeping in contact by
  telephone if you can't meet up.
- Forget guilt and aiming for 'perfect' parenting –
  it doesn't exist!

Top ten ways to deal with tantrums

1 Try to ensure you have as much relaxed, enjoyable time as possible with your child. It is bad for both of you if tensions spoil things every time you are together. Take a walk in the park or read a story together, especially if it has been a difficult day.

2 Your child needs lots of opportunities to explore safely and try new things as soon as he is on the move. Make life easier all round by moving dangerous and precious objects out of reach so that you don't constantly have to stop him. Have realistic expectations – children don't behave like adults!

3 Think about whether there are too many times you say 'no' to your child, which can lead to more defiance, and make a real effort to cut this down. Use phrases like 'We'll do it later' or 'Next time you can have a go,' instead of a blanket 'no'.

4 Keep reminding yourself of the importance of attention to your child – make sure it is mostly given for the behaviours you want to encourage. Try to ignore minor naughtiness and catch your child being good with lots of specific praise.

5 Think carefully about whether any other stresses might be affecting your child – starting in a new nursery or childcare situation, hearing parents argue or a new baby in the family can all make tantrums worse. You may need to consider working on making changes to the other situations, rather than the tantrums themselves.

6 Try keeping a diary of when tantrums happen to see if there is any pattern, and to work out the times and reasons why your child may play up more – for example, whining when he's tired.

7 Respect, accept and acknowledge your child's feelings including anger, so that they are not pushed under, ready to explode at another time. Say 'I know you're mad at me now' or 'That must have made you feel very upset.' This makes her feel you understand.

8 Provide a positive example. Try to keep calm and act in a cool, firm way, even when it is the last thing you feel. This can be difficult for many parents, but even struggling to cope is a useful lesson, rather than just giving in to anger. Out-of-control adults will always make matters worse. All the adults who care for a child should try to use a consistent approach to demands or difficult situations.

9 Use humour to take the heat out of situations. Laugh and say 'Oh no, I'm going to have to lie down on the floor too if you start that.' Tickle a child who is just beginning to go into a tantrum – it sometimes works!

10 And finally, remember: NEVER punish a child who is having a tantrum – this will always make it worse.

Index

a

ADHD (attention deficit hyperactivity disorder) 85
adult problem behaviours, links to tantrums 18–19
advance warnings 50
age of having tantrums 12, 14
Angeli, Norma 72, 85, 86
anger
    acknowledging feelings of 92
    in parents 9, 66, 87
anger tantrums 12, 17
assertive/democratic parenting 27, 70, 73
attention-seeking 33
authoritarian parenting 71
autism 85
avoidance tactics 46–7

b

baths, resistance to 38
boys 17, 26–7
'broken record' approach 58
buggies, refusing to get into 37

c

calming-down strategies 59, 84
car seats, refusing to be strapped into 37, 80
causes of tantrums 30–43
    identifying flashpoints 36–43
    tantrum triggers 32–5
Chaplin, Charlie 78
child development, normal 22–3, 47
clothes, choice of 53
consistency 58, 70
criminal behaviour in adulthood, links to tantrums 18–19

d

defining tantrums 12, 28
demands rituals 42
diary-keeping 92

difficult children 24–5
difficult situations, avoiding 48
discipline
    bringing humour into 78
    positive 74–7
distraction 37, 50, 51
distress tantrums 12, 17

e

early warning signs 48
eating, battles over 54–5
emotional overload 34
everyday battlegrounds 52–5
    choice of clothes 53
    desire for independence 55
    food and eating 54–5
exercise 47
'externalizing' behaviour 26
eye contact 65

f

Family Caring Trust 87
family rules and routines 47
feelings
    helping maturity in dealing with 84, 85
    validating your child's feelings 28
Fisher, Maggie 84, 87
flashpoints 36–43
    always wants to dawdle 38
    asks endless questions 39
    constant demands and whining 43
    demands rituals 42
    doesn't want to share 40
    is always interrupting 40–1
    just can't wait 41
    refusing to get into a buggy or car seat 37
    resists being kept clean and tidy 38
    wants to be into everything 36
food, battles over 54–5
frustration, dealing with 33

g

games, using to avoid
     tantrums 80–1
good behaviour, expecting 59

h

hair brushing, resistance to 38
happiness, feelings of 29
heading off tantrums 48–51
     advance warnings 50
     avoiding difficult situations 48
     distraction 50, 51
     early warning signs 48
     giving her some control 49
     providing a good example 49
     saying no 49
     spotting a pattern 51
health problems, tantrums caused
     by 84, 85
holding your child tightly 64–5
humour 47, 78–81
     bringing humour into discipline
     78–9
     using humour to avoid tantrums
     80–1, 93

i

ignoring tantrums, time limit for 59
'impossible' situations 35
independence
     children needing to
     prove 33, 55
     and positive parenting 70
     setting boundaries 74–5
interruptions 40–1

j

jealousy 34

l

laughter see humour
learning by example 47, 49

m

major tantrums 64–7
minor tantrums 58–9

n

natural authority 75
natural consequences 75
negative discipline 77
new baby in the family 12, 91
normal development 22–3, 47

o

older children
     having tantrums 6, 14
     helping to mature beyond tantrums
     84
oppositional behaviour 23

p

parenting skills 19, 86
parenting styles
     authoritarian parenting 71
     permissive parenting 72
     positive parenting 27, 70, 73
parents
     controlling feelings of anger 9,
     66, 87
     definitions of tantrums 28
     helping yourself 88–9
Parker, Jan and Stimpson, Jan,
     Raising Happy Children 12
patterns, spotting a pattern 51
permissive parenting 72
personal experiences 8–9
positive discipline 74–7
positive parenting 27, 70, 73
Potegal, Michael, *Temper Tantrums in
     Young Children* 12
praise 73, 76, 91
public tantrums 13, 15
     dealing with 60–3
punishment 76, 93

q

questions, asking endless questions 39

r

relaxation
exercises for toddlers 84
for parents 88
research into tantrums 16–19
rewards 75

s

sadness, feelings of 29
saying no 49, 90
setting boundaries 74–5
severe tantrums 15, 17
sharing, resistance to 40
shops, tantrums in 13, 15, 60–1
smacking 17, 76, 77
socialization 74
songs, humorous songs to avoid tantrums 80, 81
star charts 75
stress, and over-stimulation 34
strong-willed children 24–5

t

teeth brushing, resistance to 38
telephone calls, toddlers interrupting 40, 41
temperament 14, 18, 27
and adult problem behaviours 18
difficult children 24–5
tickling 81, 93
time
getting used to idea of 41
giving time and advance warnings of moving on 50
time-out 66–7
top ten ways to deal with tantrums 90–3

v

visiting friends 62–3

w

waiting, getting used to idea of 41
washing, resistance to 38
Welch, Martha, *Holding Time* 64
whining requests 43, 58, 59

Acknowledgements

Grateful thanks to all the parents and professionals who gave so generously of their time and contributed interesting ideas for me to write about.

Thanks to Aaron Hayes for patient typing of many drafts and for helping with the research.

Thanks to all of my family for managing without me on so many occasions in order to let me write this book.

Executive Editor Jane McIntosh
Editor Camilla James
Senior Designer Joanna Bennett
Designer Ginny Zeal
Production Controller Jo Sim
Picture Librarian Jennifer Veall
Photography Peter Pugh-Cook

All photographs © Octopus Publishing Group/Peter Pugh-Cook